Basic Intarsia

with Lucille Crabtree

Text written with
and photography
by Leslie Bockol

Schiffer
Publishing Ltd
77 Lower Valley Road, Atglen, PA 19310

Dedication

I want to thank my four children for their encouragement to reach out and try new and beautiful things, to achieve in areas I never dreamed possible.

Thank you, David, for introducing me to the world of intarsia. You guided and directed my hands and mind to achieve it. Thank you, Brenda, for being at my side and sharing in my enthusiasm for this work. Thank you, Jean and Randy, for all your needed encouragement to go beyond what I thought I was capable of. You all gently nudged me to continue and succeed the seemingly impossible.

May this book be an expression of my love to all of you.

Copyright © 1995
By Lucille Crabtree

Library of Congress Cataloging-in Publication Data
Crabtree, Lucille.
Basic Intarsia: with Lucille Crabtree/ text written with
and photography by Leslie Bockol.
p.   cm.
ISBN: 0-88740-727-7 (pbk.)
1. Marquetry. I. Bockol, Leslie. II. Title.
TT192.C73 1995
745.51--dc20   94-37135 CIP

Printed in China

We are interested in hearing from authors
with book ideas on related topics.

Published by Schiffer Publishing Ltd.
77 Lower Valley Road
Atglen, PA 19310
Please write for a free catalog.
This book may be purchased from the publisher.
Please include $2.95 postage.
Try your bookstore first.

Contents

Introduction

The Webster Dictionary gives this definition of Intarsia: "a wooden mosiac...inlaid into the surface; the technique of ornamenting such a surface." If we look around us, we see many things that are a form of this Italian Renaissance art form, including marquetry and inlay. However, today the art is being applied to more and more different areas, even cloth.

Traditional wooden intarsia was applied to many different articles, from walls and floor murals to furniture, mantels, and doors. First, a recessed background was carved into the subject to be decorated. Then, small mosaic tiles were inserted to form a scene or picture. These were attached with glue or mastic. The surface was then scraped to give a flat appearance, rubbed down, and finished with the same techniques used to finish fine furniture.

Then as now, wooden intarsia incorporated the use of stains and dyes. This is definitely up to the individual's taste or needs. The use of other mediums, such as stones or metal, can also be a very striking combination.

In the past, intarsia craftsmen had to go to great expense to import rare and exotic woods for their color and texture. The work itself took long hours, being a slow and meticulous craft. Although rich patrons were usually the only ones who could afford to own such intricate, expensive work, it was still very difficult for craftsmen to make a living. While the work is still very detailed and paintaking today, modern tools make it a less tedious art for the intarsia artist. The abundance of interesting woods and stains in today's hardware stores and lumber yards allows you to be as creative as you like without going to outlandish expense. And modern craft shows have proved to be an ideal market for intarsia, with customers who truly appreciate the effort and attention to detail involved in making even the simplest of pieces.

Intarsia is the art of creating an illusion, just as drawing or painting is. We who love the craft often feel that we are painting in woods. The beautiful shades, tones, colors, textures and grains are used to enhance the design, and each step in the creation of a piece is exciting. The thrill of giving it shape, of bringing it to life, makes it hard to walk away from the workshop once a piece is underway.

We in our family have always tried to design and make pieces that could be handed down from one generation to the next with pride. We like to say that they are "heritage-quality." Working with wood in this manner certainly helps give meaning to life. So enjoy each step, and experience the thrill and satisfaction of your own marvelous achievements, as you create your own intarsia.

Lucille Crabtree

Safety Equipment

This headset protects my eyes with a visor, *and* keeps sawdust out of my lungs with a vacuum fan.

A simpler solution is to wear goggles, together with a nose/mouth mask like those shown above. Be sure to read packages carefully; the labels on some masks explicitly state that they do *not* protect from wood dust.

Preparation

I also customize my belt sander before I use it for intarsia, starting with the platen (the metal backing that supports the band). I have squared these platens and filed the one on the left down to a 5/8" width, so that the sandpaper belt can bend around the metal edges as I work on round sides, especially concave curves. I also find it helpful to sand the paint off of the platen, using a 350-400 grit sandpaper. This keeps the belt running smoothly, preserving the life of the belt, and also keeps the platen from heating and causing your wood to burn. After sanding it, you can spray it with Teflon or some other product so the belt will run over the platen more easily. When you re-attach the platen, adjust it so that an index card will run easily between the belt and the platen, with just a slight drag.

Before we begin our "Baseball Sam" project, I'd like to show you the tools we'll be using, and how to get them properly set up. The first thing we need to understand, in beginning an intarsia project, is that the saw must be square. If the table is not perfectly perpendicular to the saw blade, then the pieces we cut will not be square.

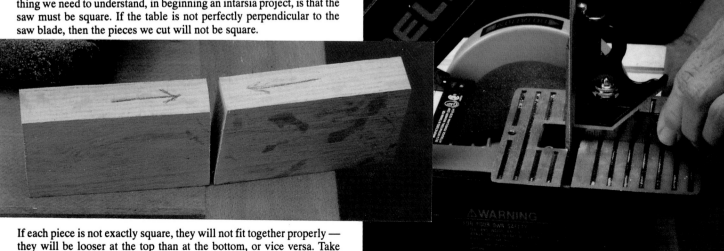

If each piece is not exactly square, they will not fit together properly — they will be looser at the top than at the bottom, or vice versa. Take plenty of time to make sure your saw is square; there will be no way to fix your pieces once you have cut them out crooked. I find that cutting a couple of 'fine-tuning blocks' is helpful; I adjust the table and re-cut them until they fit against each other perfectly. The square turning block is on the left. It makes it easy to see that the other block was out on a crooked table.

When this is done, re-attach the table. The table must then be made square to the platen. If the platen and table are not square, your pieces will mismatch, as shown here. Use a combination square and adjust the table accordingly.

Use the fine-tuning blocks shown previously to check the table again. You should do this now and then throughout your project, since the pressure of sanding will slowly make the table surface tilt. Sand the blocks again to see if they match, moving the block edge back and forth against the sanding band.

If they do not match, fine tune using light taps to the top or the bottom of the table with a mallet or a hammer. First, tighten the table. Then tap up or down with the mallet. Continue checking, tightening, and tapping until your sanded fine-tuning blocks come out perfectly square...

and perfectly matched, like these. The table is squared.

I find it helpful to cut new wooden tables for both your band saw and your band sander. This allows you to enlarge the table area, your working surface. Also, the wooden table surface (unlike the metal one) can be placed flush against the sanding band, necessary when you are working with very small pieces. Another benefit is that a wooden surface, sanded smooth and sprayed with Teflon, is better for sliding the wooden pieces you will be working with.

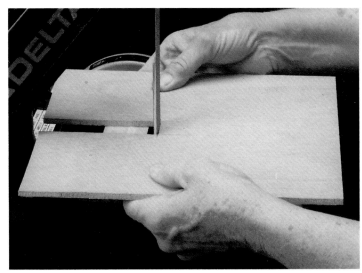

The table I am adding to the band sander here is 1/4", in a 10" x 10" square, but you can make it any size you are comfortable with. I will cut out a strip measuring 1 1/16" x 4" to allow for the band.

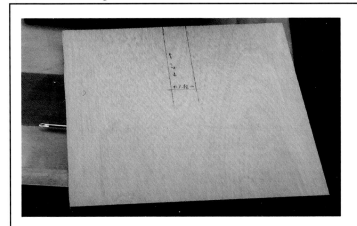

Use double-sided carpet tape on the metal table, making sure that the surface is dust-free.

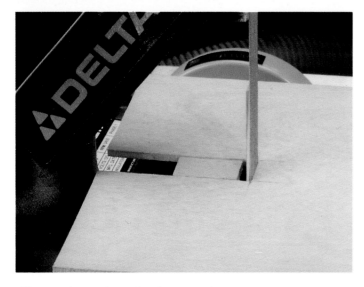

Then put the wooden surface in place, being sure to brush off any dust. Save the small cut out piece, and re-position it behind the band. This provides another useful working surface, and keeps the carpet tape below from accumulating dust.

Lay two strips of double-sided carpet tape at the front and the back of the metal table, and slide the wooden surface into place. Press down firmly. As you work, the area around the blade may get ragged. If so, turn the machine off, and pry the board off of the tape gently. Turn the machine back on, and cut a little further into the board, so that you have a fresh surface.

You can use a similar procedure for the band saw. Instead of cutting out an open strip, however, just cut halfway through your new wooden table top, which here is 15" x 21". Remove it, and then clean the metal table top thoroughly; be sure to brush off the new wooden surface too.

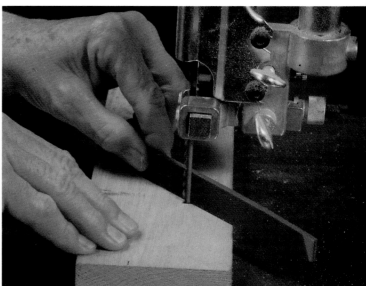

My last step in setting up my equipment is rounding the back of the saw blade, in order to make tighter turns and to help eliminate any vibrations from the blade. To do this, turn on your band saw, and partially run through a piece of wood; this will keep the blade secure, and gives you a surface to rest upon. Then, begin to rotate a metal file or other sharpening tool around the back corners of the blade. Turn off the bandsaw, and check with your fingers to see if the blade corners are rounded. Before you back the piece of wood off of the blade, be sure the machine is off; otherwise the wood can pull the blade off of the wheel.

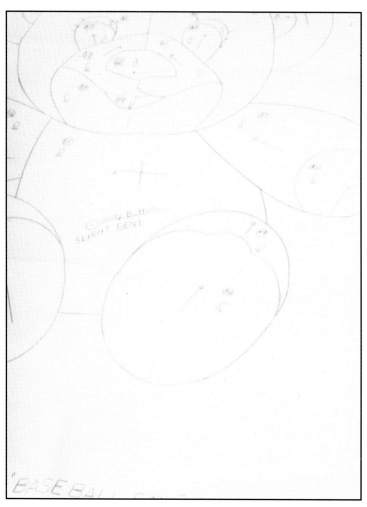

Using the Pattern

When you purchase a pattern, you will receive it in two separate layout stages: one in which all the pieces are assembled into the complete teddy bear, and one in which the pieces are disassembled and placed together according to the type or color of wood. If you Xerox the pattern to adjust the size (as you will with the reduced pattern in this book), always work from the completed, assembled pattern, not the disassembled one. If you Xerox the disassembled pieces, you will find that the copier stretches the image slightly — just enough that the pieces will not fit back together again. For this reason it is best to always work from several Xeroxed copies of the assembled bear, and cut the pieces apart yourself — that way you will KNOW that the pieces fit.

On a pattern, each outlined segment represents a separately-cut piece of wood. Each segment is marked with a letter (indicating the type or color of wood suggested for it), an arrow (indicating the direction the grain should go in), and a number (for tracking purposes). Many intarsia craftsmen find that paying attention to the varying grain directions, the knots, and the hard and soft areas of the wood greatly enhances the finished product.

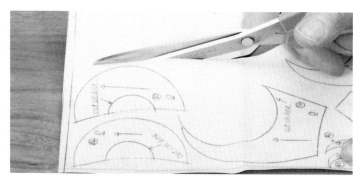

If you are working with a purchased pattern that includes a pattern-piece layout for each type of wood, you can lay each whole section down on the appropriate board...

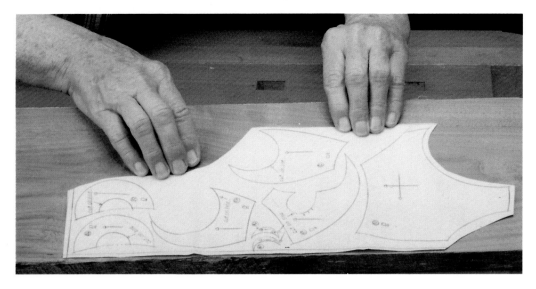

...and secure it with rubber cement or spray adhesive. Just make sure that the designer kept the grain directions consistent!

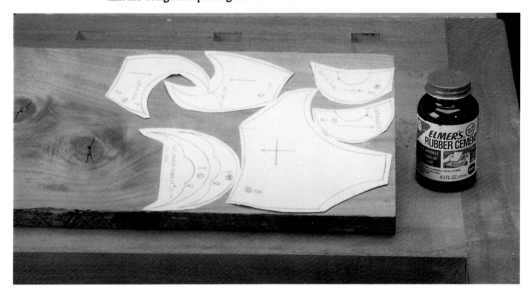

Or, you can cut it apart into separate pattern pieces to lay at your discretion. If you are Xeroxing the assembled bear from this book, this is the way you will proceed. Again, secure with rubber cement or spray adhesive.

When cutting out individual paper pattern pieces, leave at least a 1/16" — 1/8" edge around them, so that you will have room to distinctly see the line as you cut with the band saw later.

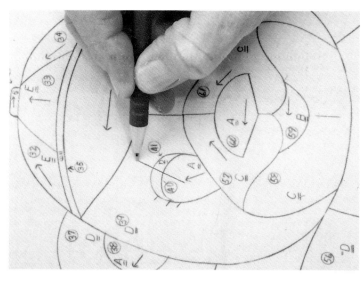

Laying Out the Pattern

A helpful hint: Small pieces, like the eye and the eyelid, are difficult to match and fit precisely when you are sizing them or fitting them together. Because the paper pattern pieces stay glued to the wooden pieces through the delicate sizing/fitting stage, it is possible to give yourself "clues" written on the paper to help guide you as you size them together. Here, on the assembled pattern, I have marked a straight red line through two small pieces that must match perfectly — the pupil (#40) and the eyelid (#41).

Be careful when you lay out your pieces: keep in mind that a single board contains many different shades of color. Do not lay a single pattern piece across a section of wood with varying shades unless you wish to achieve a contrasting color or striped effect. Plan ahead; you are painting with wood! The difference in shade between the outer edges and the middle of a board may not seem drastic now, but after the varnish is applied the difference will be very obvious. As your finished intarsia piece ages, this difference can become even more distinct.

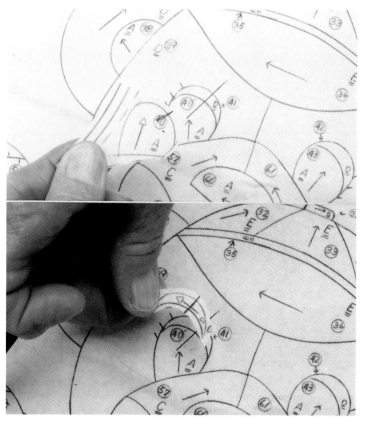

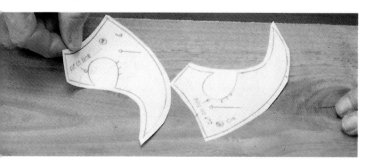

It is especially important to match grains and colors closely for paired pieces, like the two halves of the face shown here, or the ears, paws, legs, etc. When using wood colors or shades to 'paint' with for an intarsia project, consider the way light might fall on the animal or the object, making some areas darker than others. Try to coordinate the shades of wood you use.

Using a lightbox (or a sunny window), I trace these red lines from the assembled pattern onto the individual cut-out paper pieces for #40 and 41 before rubber-cementing them to their separate, different-colored boards (the pupil will go to a dark-colored board, the eyelid to a light one). Here, you can see how I have traced the red line onto the two cut-out pieces. Later, these red lines will show me how the pupil and the eyelid must be matched up in sizing and sanding after the wood is cut. This can be time-consuming, but it is easier than having to cut out brand new pieces because of a poor fit later! Remember, intarsia is about precision.

When you place the patterns for small pieces like the eyelids, you should draw in "handles." These will allow you to keep the pieces square when you are cutting them out on the band saw and sizing them on the sander. The handles should be placed on the outside curved edge, since your most painstaking work will be to carefully fit the inside curve of the eyelid to the pupil. As you will see later, you will be able to use the pupil itself as a 'handle' after the inside lid is fitted to it, when it comes time to shape the outside curve of the lid.

When you lay out the board, be aware of the knots in the wood. Pieces cut out from the knots cannot be used. Note especially where the knots fall on the reverse of the board; sometimes they go through the wood at an angle. You can either mark with a colored pencil the areas which you'll have to avoid, or you can drill a hole through the wood marking the edges of the knots; be sure to do this from both sides.

Looking at this cherry board you can see small knots, which are perfectly fine to use; many times they will enhance the intarsia piece. Plan carefully where you'd like them to appear (or not appear!).

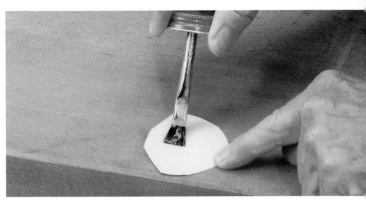

After all of the pieces for a single board have been laid in place, you can start to glue them down. Spread rubber cement evenly over the entire back of each piece,

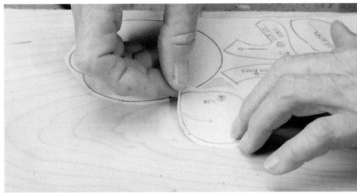

and then lay the piece down on the board.

Sometimes you will need to lay down a larger pattern piece partway....

...and glue as you press it into place.

Cutting Out the Pieces

The outside curve of the small piece has been cut outside-line; you will see all the excess left over. Since I cannot easily sand and fine-tune the inside of the big piece, I have left myself more of the small piece to work with, so that I can use it to get a close fit when I size/fit the two pieces together.

Look at these two piece from the ear. The inner curve of the large piece will be difficult to fine-tune with the band saw, so I have cut it on-line; you will see that there is not trace of the line left.

PATTERN PIECE

A   B   C

When using a band saw or scroll saw, there are three ways to cut: a) **on-line**, b) **mid-line**, and c) **outside-line**. When you cut on-line, you must be careful to cut away all traces of the line drawn on the paper, without entering any further into the wood, since this will leave you with a gap on your piece. Mid-line cutting leaves a trace of the line behind, which will allow you some room for sanding. Outside-line cutting leaves the entire line; you will use sanding to take out the remainder of the line when you fine-tune, and to smooth out any ridges left by the vibration of your blade.

On-line cutting (sometimes referred to as inside-line) is used in concave areas, corners, and other areas where it is difficult to fine-tune by sanding — where you will want to be as precise as possible on the first pass, with the band saw. The pattern frequently indicates areas where it is a good idea to cut this way.

Mid-line cutting is used in areas that are easy to fine-tune with your sander, so you can leave some leeway for fitting the adjacent pieces.

Outside-line cutting, which gives you even more leeway for fine-tuning with your sander, should be used on any piece that will not be difficult to sand. Most of the pieces for this project should be cut on the outside-line, since almost every band saw has some degree of vibration. Leaving this safety allowance gives you more room to work with the sander; Only inside very tight curves and corners should you try to do the sander's job with the saw blade.

If you think ahead and group your pattern pieces into portions of a manageable size on the board, you can then cut the board into several segments. These will be easier to handle than a long plank when you are doing more detailed cuts.

This segment of wood has the patterns for the eyelids and the left half of the face, with its concave cut-out for the eye socket.

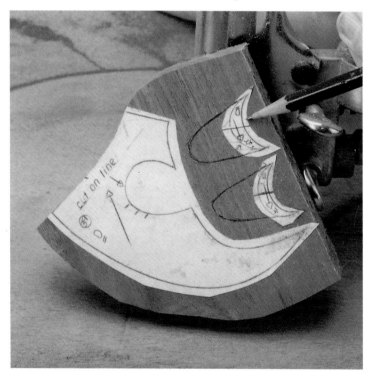

To cut out the eyelid, with its handle: First, cut the inside concave curve of the eyelid. Because this curve will be difficult to fit and sand, I will cut it on-line.

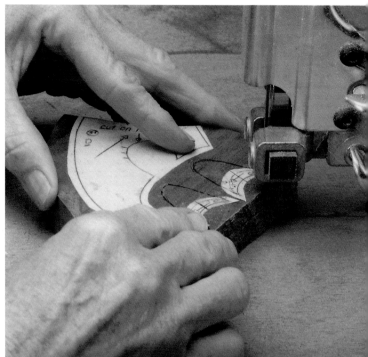

I find it helpful to focus a spotlight on my working surface, since I will need to see the lines very clearly. Some people even use a magnifying glass. Rotate the piece around the blade, just as you would on a scroll saw, but much more slowly.

The handle can be cut out very roughly, with an outside-line cut. These handles will give you something to hold onto while you sand and fit this piece, allowing you to keep the angles square. Later, they will be cut off and discarded.

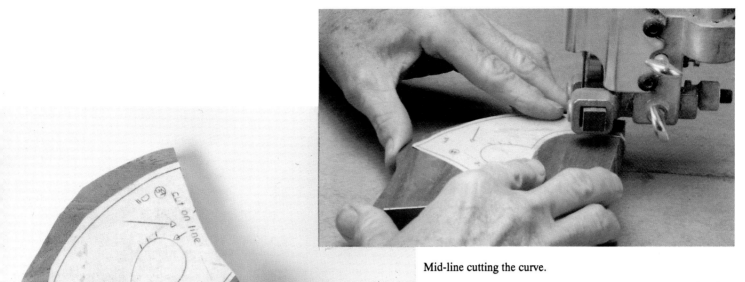

Mid-line cutting the curve.

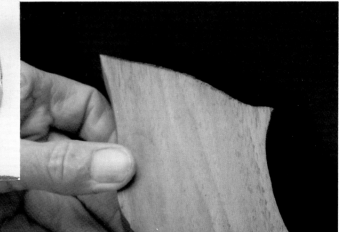

The two eyelid piece, with handles.

Cutting on a band saw or a scroll saw always leaves a fuzz on the bottom of the piece of wood. This fuzz prevents proper cutting of the next line, since it will misalign the angles, and makes it impossible to get a straight, close fit.

The first step in cutting out the left half of the face will be this curve. This should be cut mid-line, because it will be moderately difficult to size/fit by sanding (especially if you don't have a small drum sander to fit on a drill or an oscillating sander).

Take off this fuzz with a sanding block. It is also a good habit to get into to write the piece number (from the pattern) onto the back of the wood at this time, as a back up for later, when you peel off the paper.

The next step in cutting out the face is the eye socket — delicate work. It must be cut on-line, since it will be tricky to use the band sander to remove any excess wood inside such a tight concave curve.

On-line cutting the eye socket.

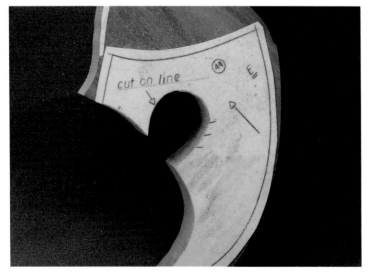

Note how closely the sides have been cut. The top, where I left too much of the line, will have to be sanded down later with a very small drum sander. If you do not have a drum sander of the right size, you can wrap sandpaper around a dowel to sand this area.

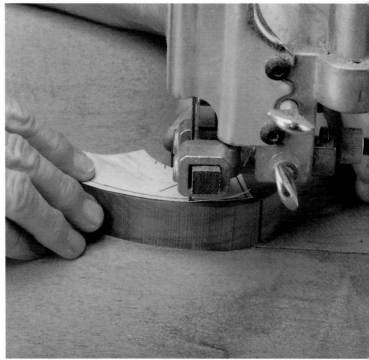

Finish cutting out the piece.

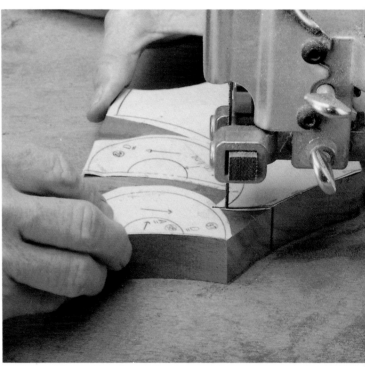

When using a band saw, remember: always shut the machine off before backing out of a cut. With a scroll saw, on the other hand, you must leave it running when you back out.

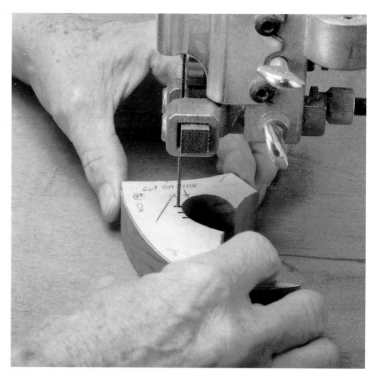

To cut out the eyelashes, make short, straight cuts. You will use the same technique to make the seams of the baseball. Because these cuts are so short, you can get away with leaving the machine on when you back out of these cuts. For the longer 'girlish' eyelashes of figures like Priscilla Bear (pictured in the gallery at the back of the book), however, you will have to shut off the blade.

Here are the finished eyelashes. Remember to sand the fuzz off the back.

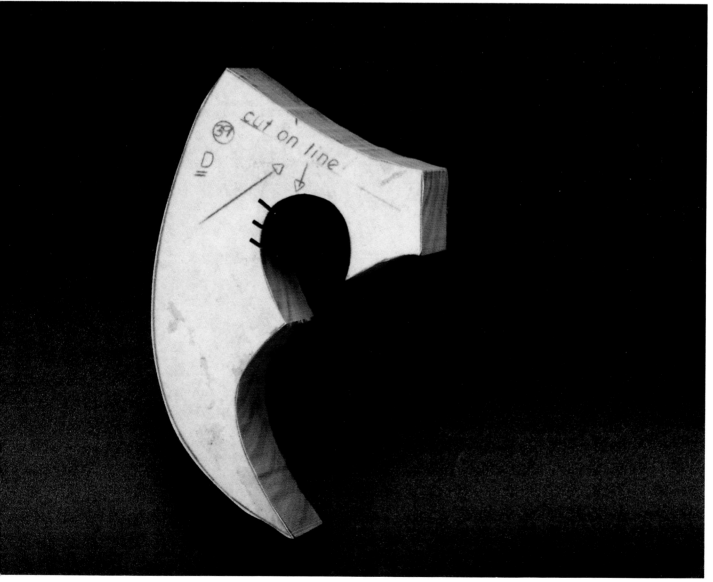

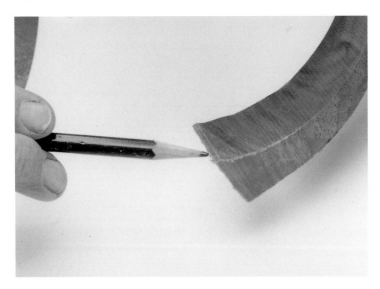

You may find that you are left with tiny up-turned "ledges" at the end of your cuts. To avoid these ledges, pause for a moment right before the end of your cuts.

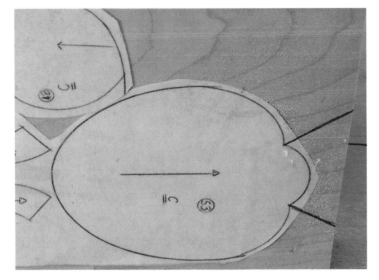

Another useful trick: when you are going to cut a piece that has several different connecting curves, like this foot, it is useful to make cuts as shown by the pencil lines here.

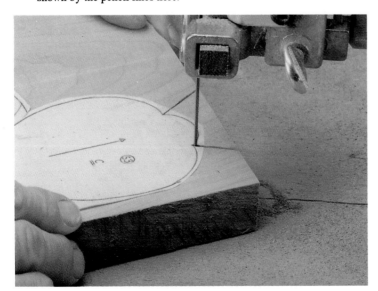

Cutting the pencilled-in lines.

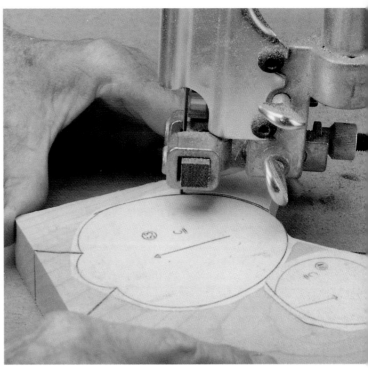

As you finish one curve (connecting with a pencil-line cut) a piece of the excess wood will fall out, leaving your blade free. Without these extra lines, you would have to shut off the machine and back out of the curved cut.

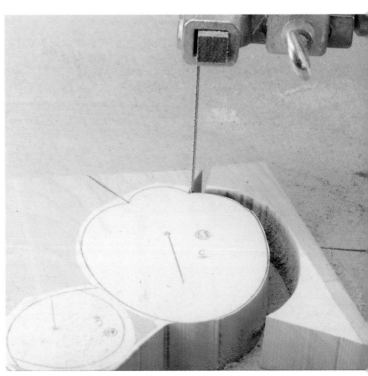

Here I have raised the arm of the band saw to give you a clearer view of this cut.

Using the three types of cutting we have discussed — on-line, mid-line, and outside-line — and the other helpful hints, you should be able to cut out the rest of the pieces for this project with the necessary degrees of precision. Remember to sand down the fuzz after every cut. It is helpful to place each cut-out piece back onto the pattern as you finish it, so that you know how far along you are with this part of the project and don't misplace anything.

Beginning to Size the Pieces

Sizing or fitting means sanding pieces down until they fit together. This takes place in two stages: the first to achieve a general fit, and the second to make sure that everything is absolutely precise. During the first sizing stage, you should try to sand the pattern line out, getting rid of the excess you left when you made the mid-line and outside-line cuts. Do not sand down to the line without continuously checking your piece against adjacent pieces, though, especially as you work with small, detailed facial pieces. It is more important for them to fit together than for you to erase all the pattern lines.

Before you begin sanding, check your band sander and platen again to make sure that they are square to the table. Re-check this periodically, since the pressure you will be exerting on it as you sand will throw it out of line. If your table is not square throughout the project, your pieces will not fit together well.

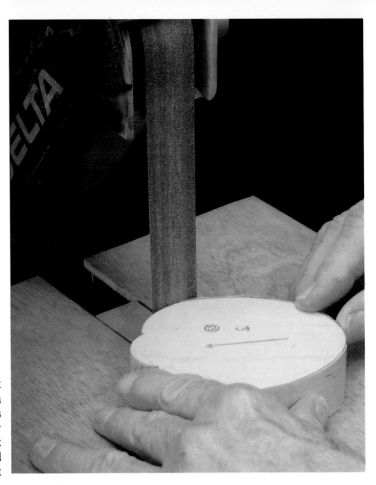

Sand the foot down to the pattern line, checking regularly to see how closely it fits.

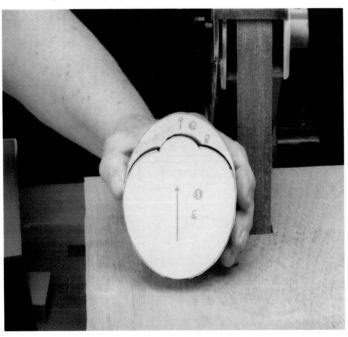

The foot and toes, before the first stage of sizing. Note the gaps between these two adjacent pieces.

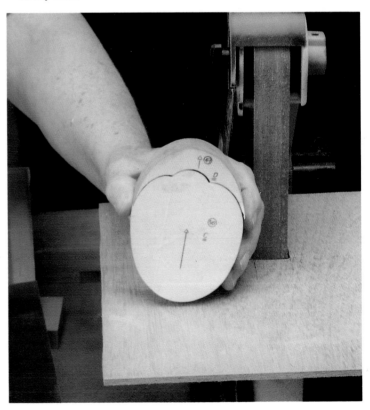

In the first sizing, you will be shooting for a closer, if not perfect, fit — something like this: the same foot and toes, after the first sizing. While some fine-tuning remains, it is fine for now.

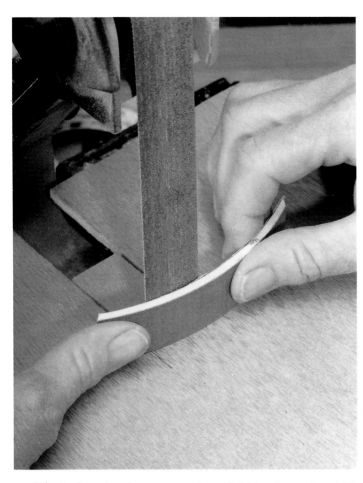

Keep in mind that the edges of pieces that do not have to match up to other pieces, like the outer edge of the bear's ear, shown here, do not need to be sanded down to the blue line if you do not so desire. The excess left here will do no harm.

It is also important that you remember to hold the piece at the middle, not at the top or the bottom...

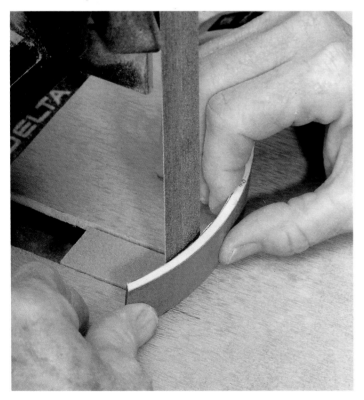

Pressure at the top or bottom will make it sand unevenly, removing too much wood from either the top or the bottom. If this happens, the piece will not fit squarely. Another block can be set or taped against the piece to keep it square and protect against tilting while sanding or sizing.

The platen, since I filed it down at the beginning, will now allow me to sand curves more easily. Take advantage of this benefit by rotating your piece around either side of the belt. You can see how the band is curving slightly around the platen as I rotate the piece.

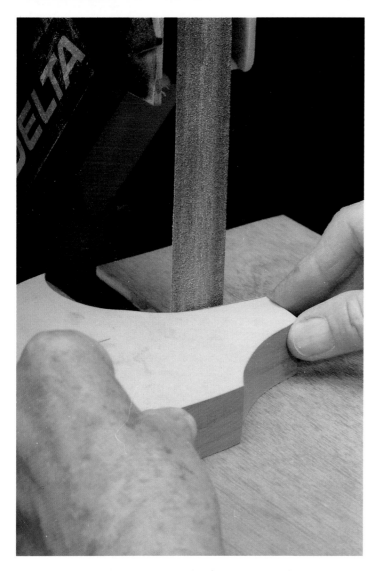

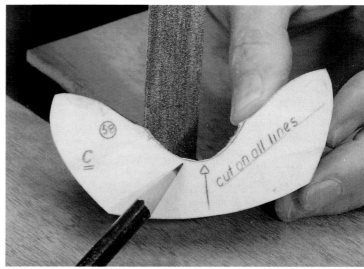

....but the center needs to be sanded with a drum sander, or by hand with a dowel wrapped in sandpaper.

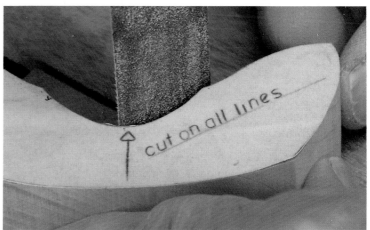

Be careful how tightly you rotate the pieces around the belt, so the belt edge does not dig into the wood, cutting a ridge into your piece. The sander, like the saw, causes some "fuzzing" — so use a sanding block to remove it, being careful not to break any important edges.

If you try to sand the center with the belt sander, it will leave ridges, because the edge of the belt will cut into the piece. And watch out! As you pay attention to one corner, the other side of the sander may be attacking another part of your piece!

This piece, the bear's chin, cannot be sized using the belt sander alone. The sides of the mouth curve can easily be sanded with the belt...

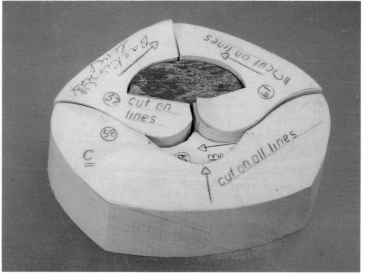

If you work in units, it is much easier to fit the pieces together. This unit consists of the nose, mouth, chin, and cheeks. I find it very useful to think of the project as a number of major units that work together.

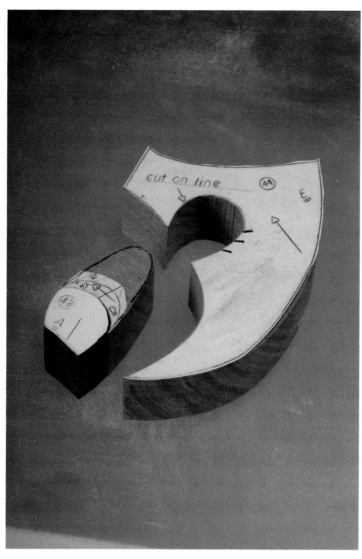

Another important unit consists of the eye, eyelid (with handle), and face. First, I will sand the face piece down to the mid-line point of the pattern line,

Once they fit perfectly, tape the eye and the eyelid together on the top **and** on the bottom, and return to the band saw to cut off the handle.

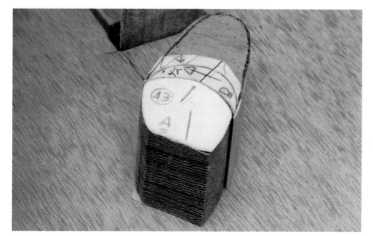

and then closely fit the pupil into the curve of the eyelid (and handle). You can see here the red lines that I drew while the pattern was intact, and then traced onto my paper pieces; as I fit and sand now, I will be very careful to match up these important guidelines. The handle is crucial in this step; without it, the eyelid is too small to sand without risking your fingers, and is very difficult to keep square to the belt. Sand out the pattern line.

Now that the two pieces of the eye have been attached with tape, you can use the eyeball as a new handle as you sand the top of the lid, where the old handle used to be.

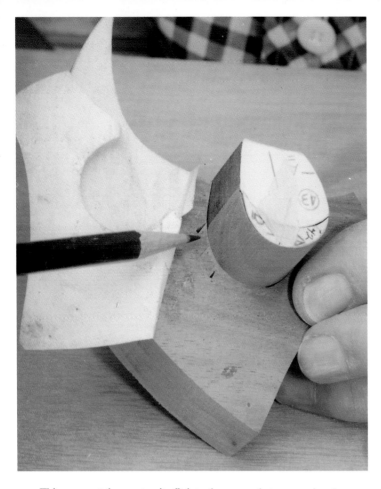

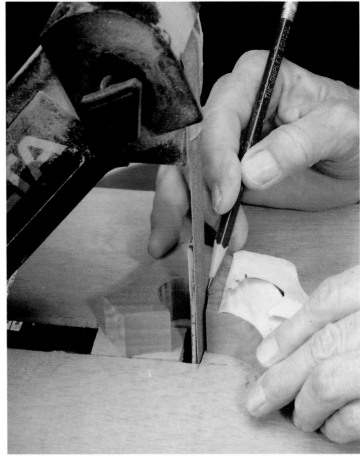

This one spot does not quite fit into the eye socket, preventing the eye unit from slipping into place. Never force a piece into its spot; pieces should be snug, but easy to slide smoothly in and out. If you force piece together too tightly, you will have trouble later, as moisture is absorbed by your finished piece; this can cause the wood to split and crack. This spot will need to be sanded with the belt sander. Mark the trouble-spot with a pencil line...

Another tight spot on the eye unit, which I have marked with a pencil, can be taken care of by lightly sanding the side of the eye socket. As we've discussed before, sanding inside of concave curves like the eye socket can be tricky; that is why we cut it closely, on-line, before. However, sometimes it is possible to reach some parts of the curve with the belt sander. Rather than pressing hard against the sander, I only touch it lightly, what I call 'feathering'. I have peeled the paper back slightly to get a clearer view of the wood.

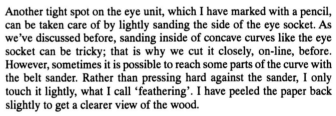

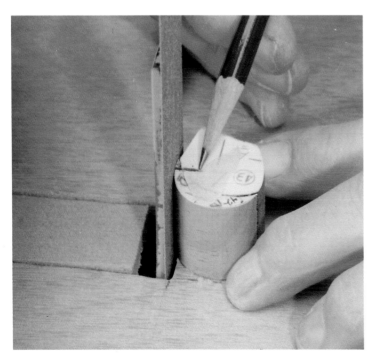

and then move the piece to the sander to continue sizing.

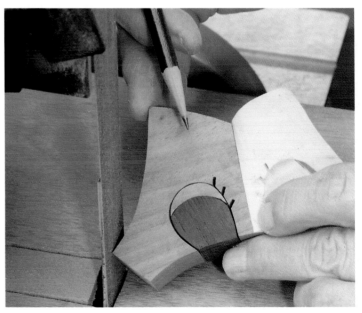

See how smoothly the eye unit fits together now; there are no gaps. Now you can continue with the first fit/sizing stage for the rest of your pieces, sanding away the pattern line for a reasonably good fit.

The Final Sizing

You can see that I have transferred the piece number — 50 — to the bottom of this paw piece. Check the bottom before you proceed, to make sure that any ragged or fuzzy edges have been smoothed down, or else they may distort your fitting — they make it appear as if there is a significant amount of wood that needs to be removed with the band sander, when all that is really necessary is a quick, feathery swipe with a piece of sandpaper. Any dust or debris along the side edges can cause the same distortion; use a tack cloth or a soft brush to make sure the edges are clean. Try to keep your workbench as clear of dust as you can.

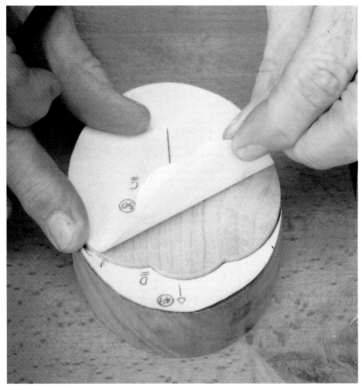

When you are ready to start the final sizing of a piece, it is time to remove the paper pattern. This allows you to get a better view of the wood's fit. Make sure you transfer the piece's number (written on the paper pattern) onto the back of the wood, so that you can find its proper placement. Another important reason for marking the back of each piece is so that you can tell the back from the front once the paper has been removed — with symmetrical pieces, it is almost impossible to guess which side is the top!

Use a belt eraser to remove the rubber cement or spray adhesive from the top surface of the wood. Erase in the direction of the grain; if you erase cross-grain, you will work the residue into the wood.

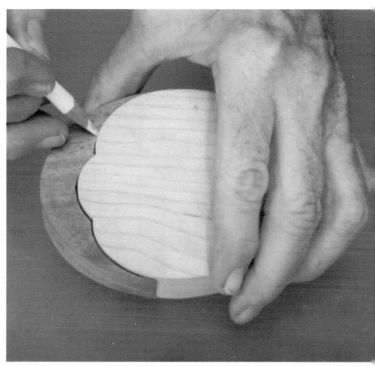

Here I see four spots that I must sand down. Mark every trouble spot on the wood with a pencil (white pencil on dark wood, black pencil on light wood) so that you can clearly see the spots you intend to sand down for your fitting.

Place the two piece to be fitted together onto a light table. If you see light shining through any gaps, you will know that there are bumps keeping the pieces from achieving a perfect fit. These bumps must be sanded away.

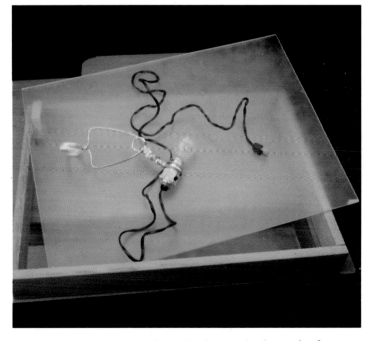

It is easy to improvise a light table: I use a simple wooden frame, a sheet of clear plastic (sanded down with the vibrating sander to make it 'frosted'), and a light bulb fixture.

I will feather (lightly sand) these on the 1" band sander, continuing to check them until I get the proper fit. Be careful — it is very easy to over-sand these spots, removing too much wood. If this happens, you can throw off the alignment of the entire piece, and sometimes you will need to make an entirely new replacement piece. When the light table reveals no gaps between the paw and the toes, you have a snug fit. Place the paw unit into position on the pattern to keep things organized, tape two ways across the seam and move on to the next piece!

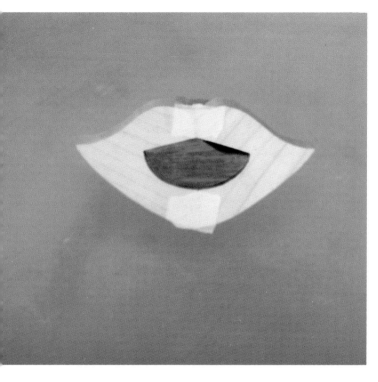

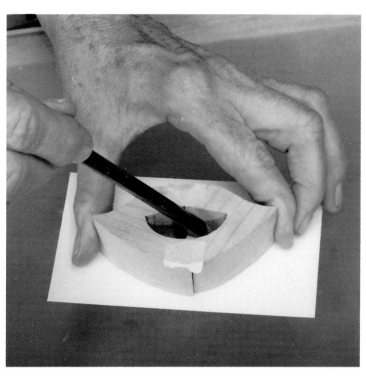

Be careful that you do not oversand a piece. Here I have oversanded the inside nose piece. There is no way to make these pieces fit anymore. In situations like this, the best bet is to recut a new inside nose piece to fit.

...and trace a new paper pattern piece.

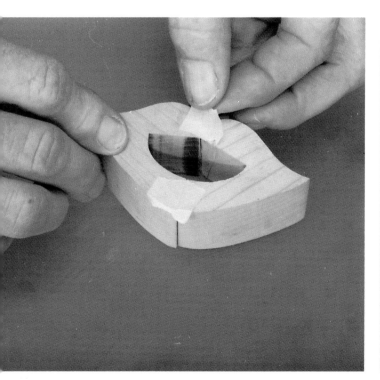

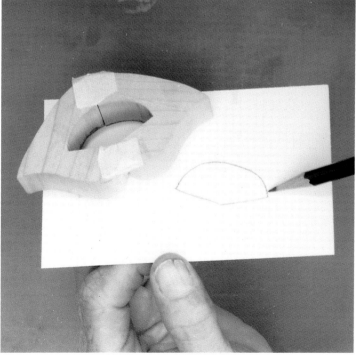

To do this, lay snout pieces back on diagram tape together and tape the snout pieces together...

Glue this to a fresh piece of wood and cut out a new nose using an outside-line cut, leaving a lot of extra room. This will give you leeway for sanding and sizing.

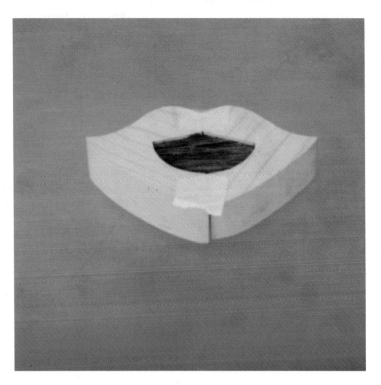

Here you have a new nose, a perfect fit.

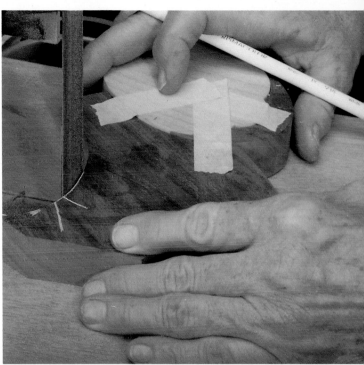

As you size other adjacent pieces, the taping will allow you to move the entire unit to and from the sanding table without having to reassemble it each time. This is especially helpful when a new piece must fit perfectly against **two** other adjacent pieces; if you tape the adjacent pieces together, you can sand them as if they were one.

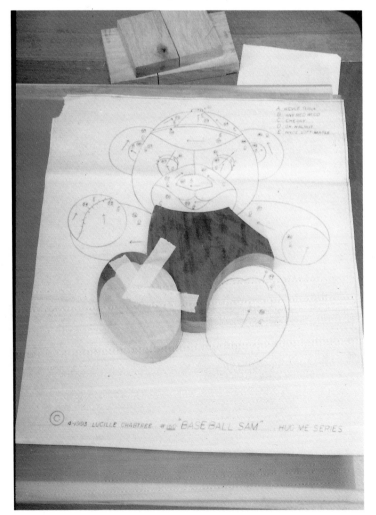

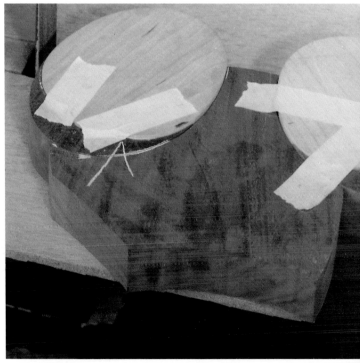

V-marks and cross hatches (like the red marks I used earlier in the eye-unit) will help you fit the pieces back together again after sanding down the bumps you marked. Now you can finish fitting all of the pieces together!

As you gradually get different segments of your figure sized and fitted, place them back on the pattern in units. I find it helpful to tape them together, to avoid shifting as I fit new pieces in.

Making Lifts and Backboards

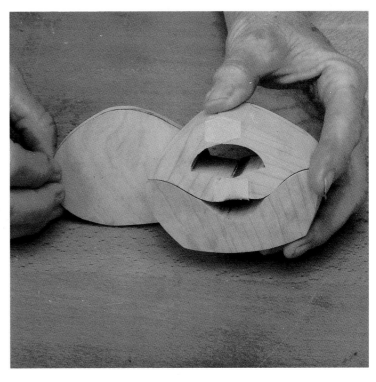

Cut inside your traced line about 1/16" to 1/8" — it does not have to come **exactly** up to the edges of the unit. This piece will eventually be glued beneath the muzzle, to give it some "lift"....

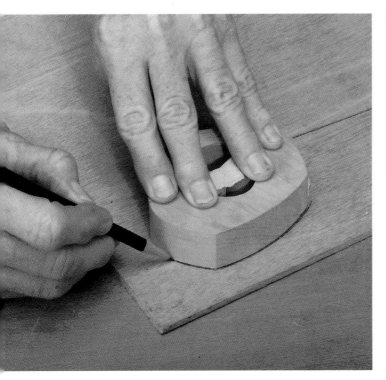

To add some extra depth to the finished figure, I want to make a few features stand out a little higher than the rest — in this bear, the mouth and muzzle unit, and the eyelids. To make the mouth and muzzle pieces — pattern numbers 57 to 61 — project slightly out of the main body of the bear, I will trace and cut a matching piece of 1/4" plywood.

...in the completed face. You can make two very small lifts for the eyelids this way if you like, but a broken piece of toothpick or a fragment of scrap wood will work just as well, or you could glue the lids to the pupils in a raised position (securing them with a rubber band while they dry) before putting the entire figure together. Just be sure that you make all your lifts **before** you start the shaping stage — that is, rounding off the top edges to give the finished figure a soft, contoured, three-dimensional look. You will need to know the relative heights of your pieces — lifts included — to make your decisions about shaping.

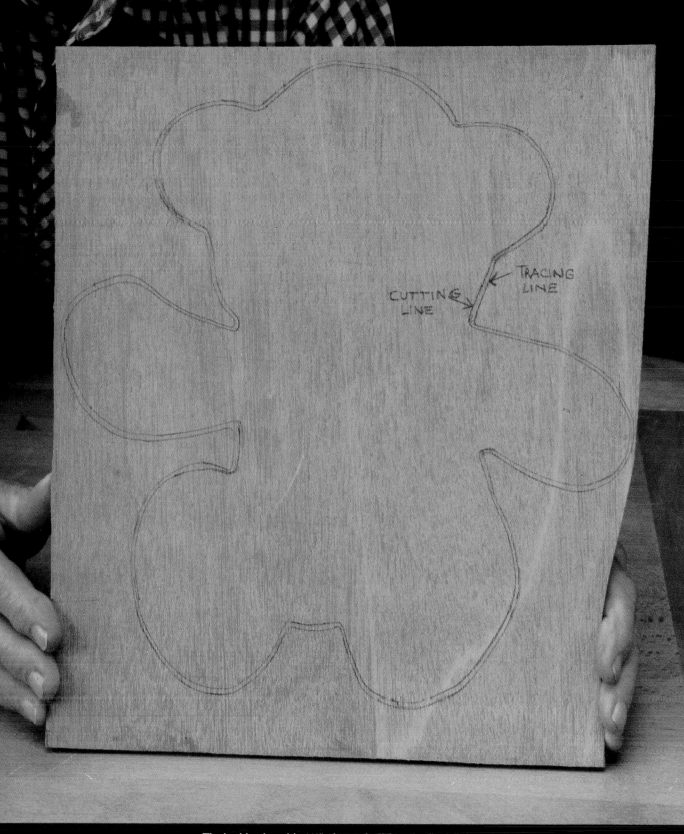

The backing board is 1/4" plywood. When the final fitting of all the pieces is complete and they are taped together on the pattern, you can move the whole assembly to the plywood and trace around it. Inside the tracing line about 1/16" to 1/8" you will draw a cutting line. By cutting the backing board smaller than the size of the intarsia piece, you create a nice overhang.

Before cutting out the backing board, hold the belly piece-numbered "51" on the pattern-in place and...

trace around it. This is the first piece that you will glue down when you begin the final stage of your project, and the rest of the pieces will be fitted around it. This key to placement will make it much easier to complete your final arrangement of the pieces.

Cut the backing board on the cutting line and round the edges with the
band sander. Spray paint the back.

Shaping the Pieces

Shaping the pieces with the belt sander gives them the rounded, full look that makes intarsia so beautiful. You can see the difference between the flat, unshaped belly and leg pieces here and the rounded pieces on the finished piece next to it.

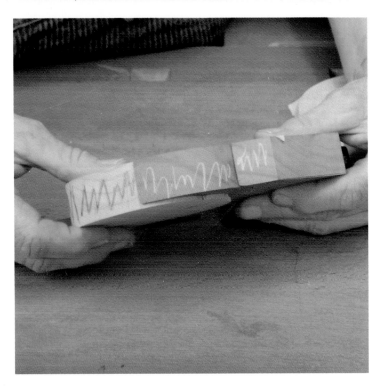

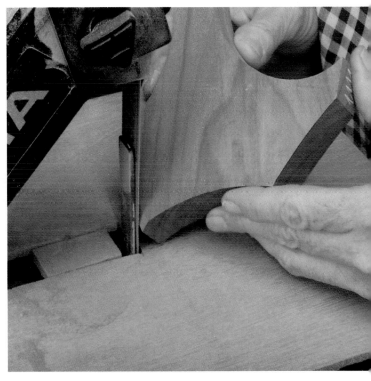

To help guide you through the shaping process, use pencils to mark all the edges that will be visible in the completed figure—the edges you traced to get the outline of the bear for the backboard. This entire outside edge of the bear will be sanded smooth—from top to bottom of the edge. It is important that you clearly mark the edges to be sanded this way; if you sand smooth the **inside** edge —the edges that join adjacent pieces together, which you were so careful to fit/size precisely—you will ruin the fitting that you have already completed. Here, you can see that I have marked with pencil the edges that **will** be completely sanded. These marks should not be removed until the bear is completely shaped. The segment on the right is not pencil-marked, since it is not an outside edge; an adjacent piece has already been fitted to be placed next to it.

I start to round the edge, using a medium-grade sandpaper. You may prefer to keep the platen in,

but I prefer to remove it. This gives me greater flexibility as I shape.

To begin shaping, I will slope the 'hip sockets' of the body below the edges of the feet and the toes. This will give the illusion that the feet are out in front.

as you can see here.

Rounding without the platen.

I am sanding this down fairly far into the piece, because I want a gentle slope...

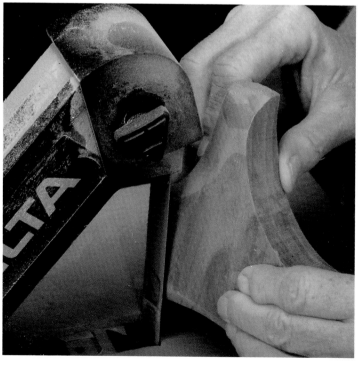

When you are sure that the edges are rounded smoothly and evenly, with the depth and slope that you want,

check it against the adjacent pieces. You can see here that I have sanded the hip socket more at the bottom to make the bear's belly taper off, as if it were rounding underneath him. It is higher at the top of his foot,

and lower at the bottom.

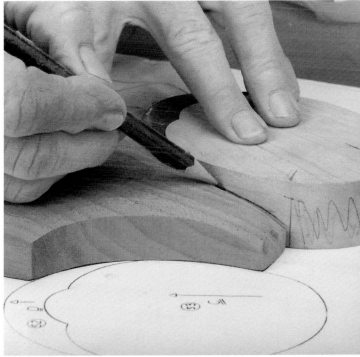

Once the hip edge of the body has been shaped, I mark the adjacent area of the foot. Be sure that the pieces are fitted together tightly, as they will be in the finished pieces, and trace the height of the hip...

To show how deep into the edge of the foot you can shape. Here, you can see that the area above the line must be rounded. Do not sand at **all** below the line. Remember to check these pieces against the pattern and against each other.

...and then on the inner edge, where the toes meet the foot.

You will notice here that the light wood (the foot) stands somewhat higher than the dark wood (the toes). I have done this to create a little more depth in the foot piece. If you choose to make any of your pieces uneven like this, you can cut off a slice with a band-saw, or use a thinner board to start out with. If you cut off a slice, be sure you take it off the **top**, not the bottom. If you remove the layer from the bottom, you risk making the piece stand unevenly, and all the squaring you did will be wasted. You may find it helpful to remove some excess this way before you start shaping a piece with the sander.

This part of the toe piece sits adjacent to the hip socket of the body. I have already traced a line indicating how deeply I can shape this segment, so I start my sanding. First, on the outer edge, where the toes meet the body at the hip...

This part of the toe piece will be on the outside edge of the completed, assembled bear; you can see the white pencil marks I made earlier to indicate this. I will now draw a line in freehand to show how deeply I would like to round this edge; it can be as deep as you like it.

The entire white-marked outside edge will need to be sanded later, to get rid of the pencil marks and to give it a smooth, finished look, but all I want to do at this stage is to round it to the depth of my freehand mark.

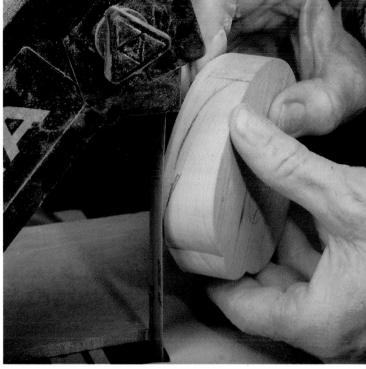

...and I proceed to shape it.

When I have completely rounded the inside of the curved toe piece, I fit it back up against the foot piece. Now I can mark the foot with a line where they meet, so that I know how deeply to round this edge...

Then I shape the edge of the foot that will be seen on the completed bear, marked previously with a black pencil. I can shape it to any depth I like, though it ought to coordinate with the outside edge of the toes that I shaped earlier.

Now, still using the medium sanding belt, I lightly sand around the edges that will be seen on the assembled bear, removing the pencil marks and any ridges that the band sander left during the sizing stage. At this stage, you should generally hold the piece vertically against the belt...

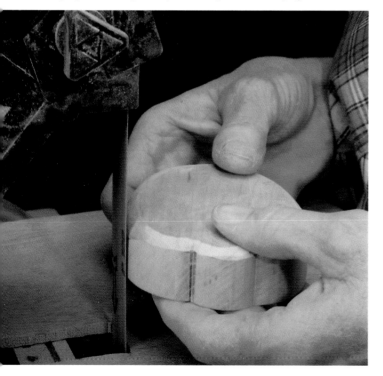

rather than horizontally. Vertical sanding will remove the grooves more easily, taking no more wood off of the piece than necessary.

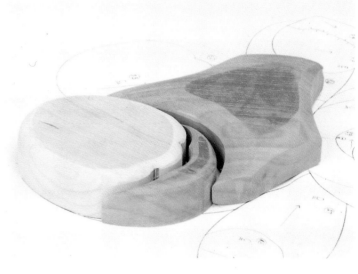

The secret to three-dimensional intarsia is reducing one edge below another,

as I did here...

...and here.

These pictures of a finished piece will show you how I have chosen to shape some of the trickier details. Here you can see how the high outer edge of the ear slopes down into the face.

You can see here how much depth can be added with this just a little extra effort. This view also shows the slope of the ear.

The eyelids are raised with lifts, as discussed earlier. To get them to stand out, I can either glue a small fragment of wood to the bottom to act as lift — a piece of broken toothpick will do — or I glue the lid to the eyeball in a raised position, securing them with a rubber band while the glue dries. They require only a slight rounding.

See how the muzzle has been given extra emphasis with the lift I made earlier. Note that the curve is gentler at the top, where the muzzle blends into the face, and sharper at the bottom, where the chin drops off into the neck. Also note the tilt of the nose, high at the top...

The tongue slants sharply back into the mouth.

...and low at the bottom.

For the most part, the joins of the bear's body will be gently rounded...

The brim of the baseball cap is a relatively even curve.

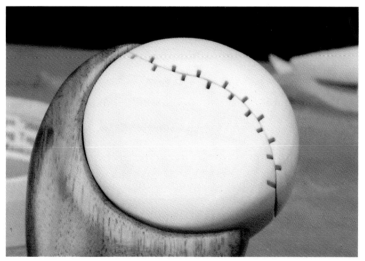

...except for the baseball seam, which will be flat. To finish the shaping stage, I go over each piece again with the sanding belt. This time I use a 320 grit paper; this will make the finishing stage much easier.

Finishing the Pieces

The bottom of this bear has been shaped and finished; the top has yet to be finished. You can see the difference that finishing makes: the bottom looks satiny and the grain directions are very clear, while the top still looks rough, with burn marks from the band sander and curves that are something short of smooth.

Here is the face, shaped, but not 'finished'. In the finishing stage, I use 220-grit paper on a vibrating sander to smooth out the shaping I have just done even though I ended up with a 320 grit belt. Try to remove any ridges, burns, or rough spots, so that you will only have to do very light work when you are doing the last bit of sanding by hand.

Try to move the vibrating sander over the piece in the direction of the grain to give smoother and rounder edges and top.

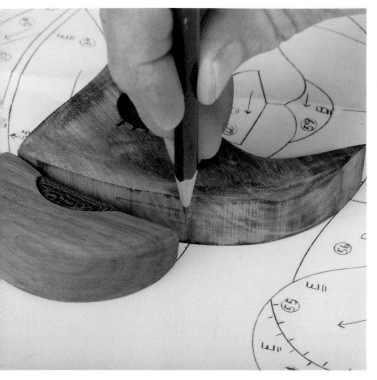

Just like during the shaping stage, it is important NOT to use the vibrating sander on the bottom edges of pieces which fit precisely against adjacent pieces; you will ruin the fitting and the squareness that took so much time to acheive. To determine what parts of each piece's edge will need to be finished with the vibrating sander, lay the pieces back onto the pattern one by one with their adjacent pieces, and use a pencil to mark different segments. On parts of the edge that do not fit against other pieces — the pieces that will be the outside of the completed bear — you will have to sand the entire edge, to eliminate the roughness that might mar the outside of your completed project. To the right of the heavy pencil mark is the edge of the cheek, which will be showing when the bear is assembled. On this segment, I must use the vibrating sander to finish the entire edge, top to bottom.

The top half of the edge, however, should be sanded, since it rises above the ear. It **will** be seen when the piece is assembled, and sanding it will **not** affect the fit of the face and the ear.

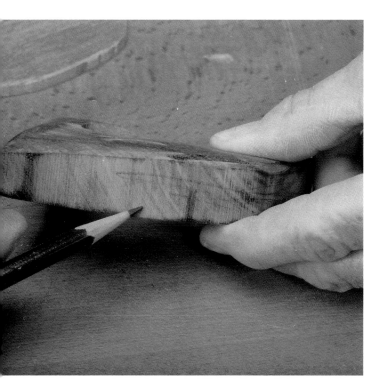

But to the left of the heavy pencil mark, the face will be joined to the ear. The bottom half of the edge must not be touched; it has got to stay fitted as it is.

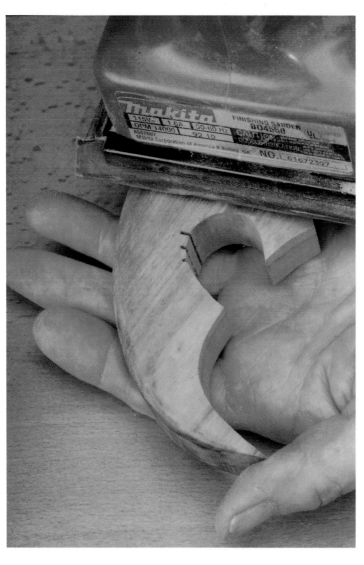

Here I am smoothing the top surface,

Once you've determined which areas must be left untouched, use the vibrating sander to finish the rest.

and I smooth the rounded edges. Even though the 220 paper is rougher than the 320 I used on the belt at the end of the finishing stage, it will provide a smoother finish on the vibrating sander. Once you start using this tool, you will quickly get an idea of how much you can do with it.

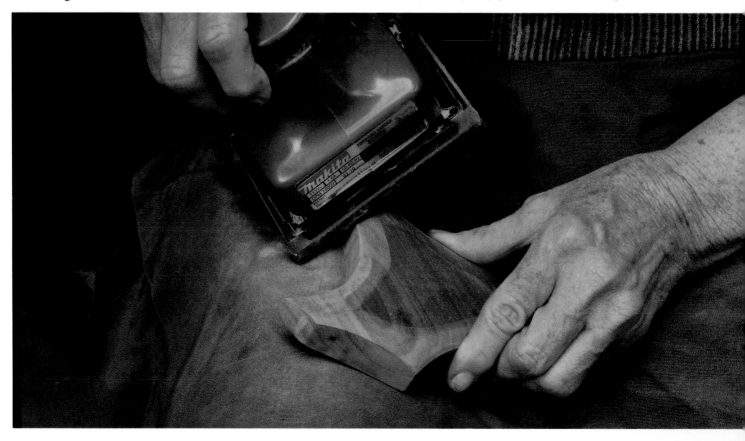

Sanding by Hand

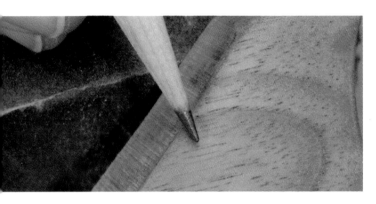

As I finish with the vibrating sander on each piece, I examine it under a strong light to find scratches that need to be removed. Here I notice some faint scratching running across the grain, which you can see if you look closely. Even scratches as minor as these will be glaringly obvious once I varnish a piece, so it is important that I search for them carefully.

Always re-check to make sure the scratches have been completely removed. Sand in the direction of the grain, or you will simply be putting **new** scratches in to replace the ones you just removed.

I mark these surfaces with a pencil, and use a square of paper or a sanding block to remove the pencil marks, taking the scratches with them.

Next, brush the sawdust off of the piece (or use a tack cloth to clean it), and you are ready to start its final hand-sanding.

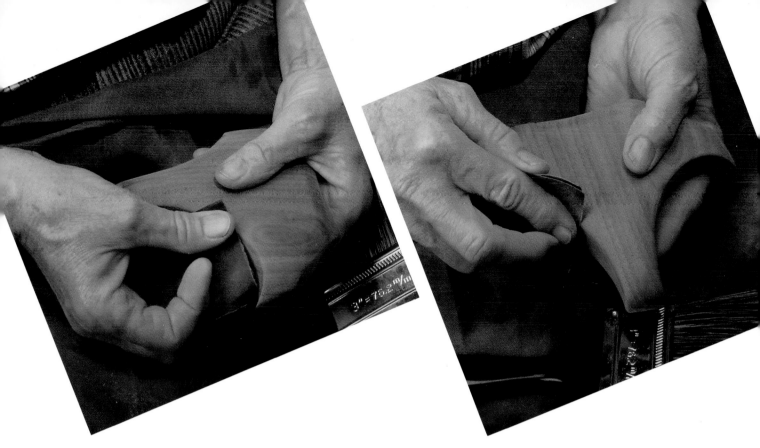

Again, I use a 220-grit paper, though after a first swipe you can move up to a finer grit to get a more satiny surface. The first step in hand sanding is to soften all the edges — 'breaking' them. You should do this before you go on to the flat top surfaces, so that your edge-work doesn't put new scratches into an already-smooth top.

After you've smoothed the top, you'll need to do a final stroke, across the top surface and then rounding over the edge. This eliminates any scratches or tiny ridges you may have made while breaking the edge.

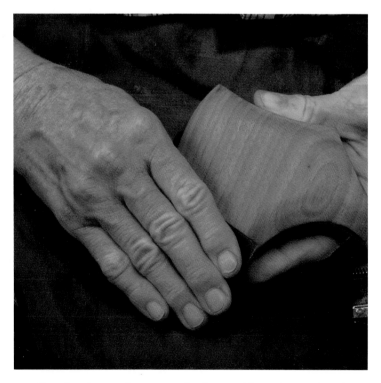

Once the edges are done, you can begin to sand the top in smooth strokes. As always, move in the direction of the grain, and get a new piece of sandpaper whenever necessary. Keep an eye out for any scratches that may still be hidden in the wood.

Brush off the piece, and move on to the next! After they are all done, you are ready for the varnishing.

Varnishing

Use a wipe-on gel varnish to add gloss to your pieces. I use a foam brush, but a soft cloth also works well. The varnish serves as a sealer, and helps prevent moisture from entering your completed piece and damaging the wood.

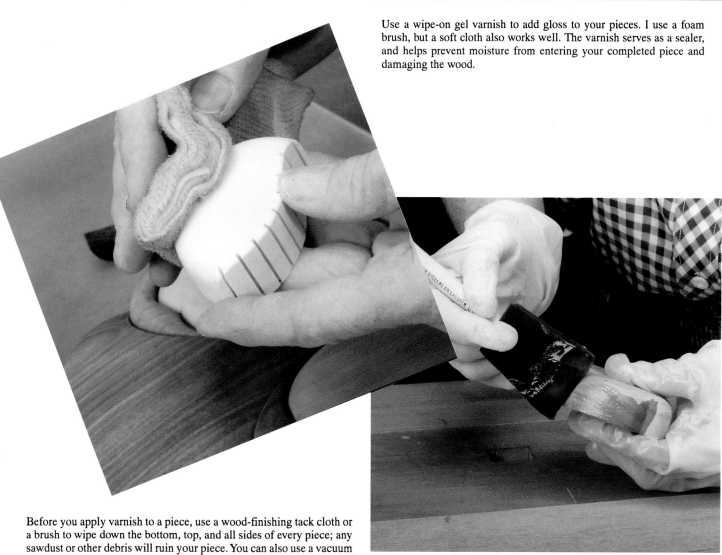

Before you apply varnish to a piece, use a wood-finishing tack cloth or a brush to wipe down the bottom, top, and all sides of every piece; any sawdust or other debris will ruin your piece. You can also use a vacuum to do this. Many people use an air blower, but this can drive the dust and small splinters into your skin, so be careful. No matter which method you use, be sure that all the pieces are clean before you begin to varnish.

Coat the sides and the top, but not the bottom. Some varnish is bound to get on the bottom, and this will have to be sanded off later.

The varnish can be put on in a thick coat. I prefer to varnish 3 or 4 pieces at a time, and then wipe them down together. If you wait too long, and the thick layer of varnish starts to harden before you get around to wiping it down, there is an easy solution: apply another light coat of varnish over the top, and let it sit for just a few seconds. This will soften the bottom layer, and then you can wipe them both off.

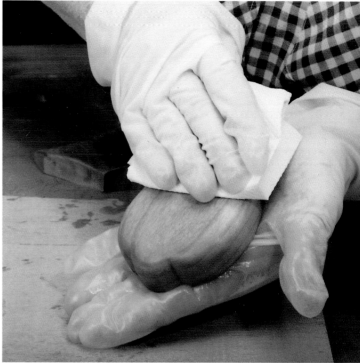

Then wipe the top, in the direction of the grain.

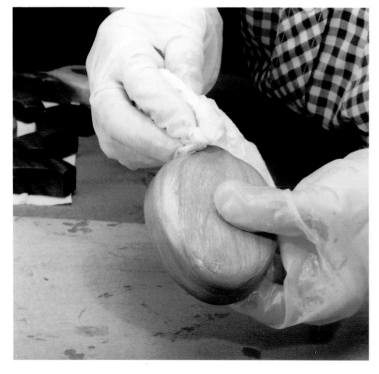

First wipe around the edges...

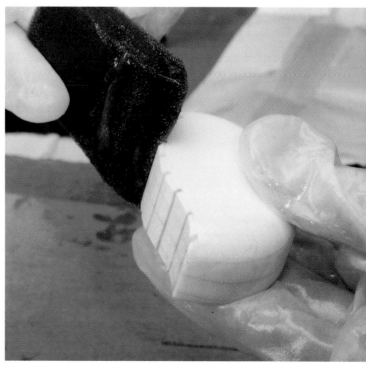

Be sure to get varnish in even the smallest crevices. If you forget to put finish on the inner cuts, like the baseball seams shown here or the eyelashes, it will show up on your finished piece.

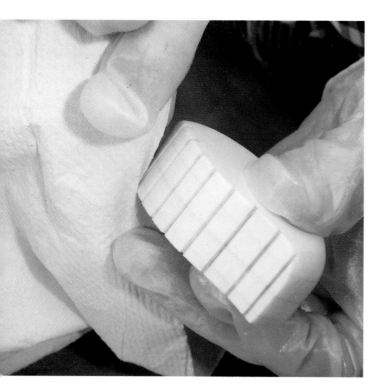

Sometimes I use a sharply-creased paper towel to run the varnish through the length of the cut, top to bottom. Really, you only have to do this for the first coat of varnish.

See how beautifully the varnish brings out the color of the wood. This is bloodwood, a dense red wood I chose to use for the details of the baseball hat and the tongue. Remember, you can use any woods you like for your own project; just pay attention to grain and color, so that your finished piece has the look of something 'painted with wood'.

Notice how small nicks in the wood will show up clearly when the varnish has been applied; there is a dent in the edge of the hat brim. If you dent a piece by dropping it or banging it against something hard, you may want to re-cut a new one, or repair and re-varnish it.

Baseball Sam, before he takes his final form. After all the pieces have
been varnished, feather across them with 400-600 grit sandpaper, in the
direction of the grain. You will need to coat these pieces with 4 to 6
coats of varnish (drying time will vary depending on the brand you
choose; read the directions on the can). Lightly sand between each coat.

Clean-Up

To do this, I will make a special sandpaper board, using a piece of sandpaper, a piece of board, and rubber cement or spray adhesive.

Invariably, some varnish will get on the back of the pieces. This will interfere with gluing the pieces to the backboard, so it must be removed.

I spread the back of the paper with glue (or spray it with adhesive according to the directions on the can)...

and lay it down. Let it dry.

Rub the bottom of each piece against this board to remove any varnish that made its way onto the bottoms of your pieces. After you've cleaned them all this way, you can begin to lay the pieces down on your backboard.

Assembling the Project

Starting with the body piece, lay the bear onto the backboard. This is a dry run — do not use glue yet! It is important to make sure one last time that everything fits.

Previously, you traced the outline of the body piece onto your backboard. As you prepare to glue the bear into place, you will be starting with this outline.

Remember the lift beneath the muzzle!

I assemble the bear in units — it is easier to control the fit if you do not need to handle all the small pieces separately at this stage.

Once the board has been properly cut and touched up, I use Titebond II wood glue to attach the body piece. I use Titebond II only for this piece, because I need a glue that will seal quickly here. For the other pieces, I need a glue that will let me shift them a little once they are down; I use Elmer's Carpenter's Glue or the regular Titebond glue, both slower-drying glues.

Looking at every side of the figure from a slight angle, I see that the backboard sticks out in two spots — the end of the paw, and underneath the arm. I will need to cut the board down in these places.

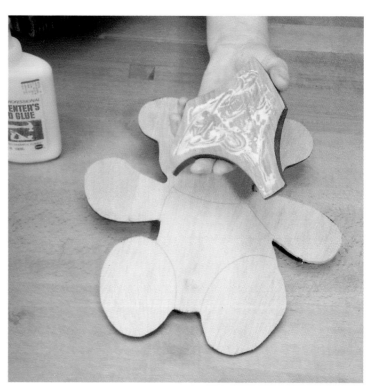

Cover the piece evenly, but not thickly, and don't worry about pushing the glue all the way to the edges. If the glue is too thick or too close to the edge, it could ooze out and ruin the fit and the look of the picture. If glue oozes out, take the piece up and wipe its sides down with a wet cloth. Be sure to get it completely clean.

54

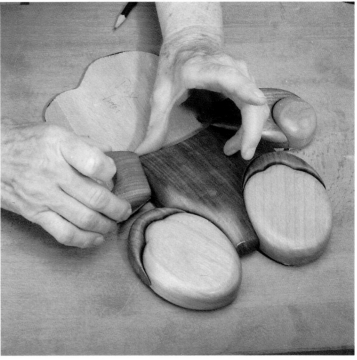

Place the body piece down, making sure to align it perfectly with the lines drawn on the backboard. Glue and let sit up.

pressing them closely up against the solidly-glued body piece.

Glue the other pieces into place,

Glue the muzzle lift into place; remember to use a glue that will allow you some time to shift the piece around as it is drying.

Coat the top of the muzzle lift with glue...

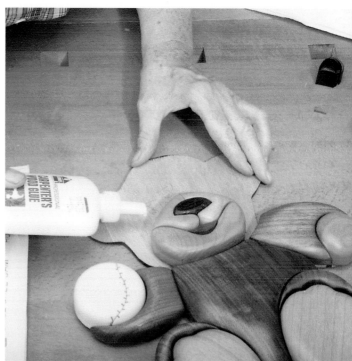

Spread glue over the rest of the backboard,

...and glue down the muzzle pieces.

And lay the rest of the pieces down, except for the eyes and eyelids, and the button on the top of the baseball cap. All of these pieces need to be settled in their proper places before the glue sets up.

I have already explained how to make a wooden lift for the muzzle or the eyelids, but this time I think I will use yet another method to make the eyelids stand out a little higher. I have decided to use epoxy or another fast-drying glue to attach the lid directly to the eyeball, with about a 1/8" gap at the bottom, so that the top of the lid projects that same height.

I have placed plywood scraps to serve as braces underneath the cap edges, since they do not have enough support from the backboard to keep them steady while they dry. I will epoxy the button to the top of Baseball Sam's cap, and (after two or three hours) he's ready to play ball!

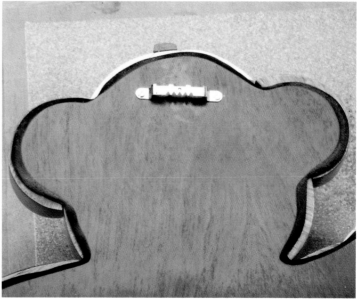

As I discussed before, another way to achieve this is to glue a small piece of wood (a scrap, or even a broken piece of toothpick) as a lift to the bottom of the eyelid piece. Once the epoxy is dry, you can insert the eyes...

As the last step, attach a hanger from the back

The Finished Projects

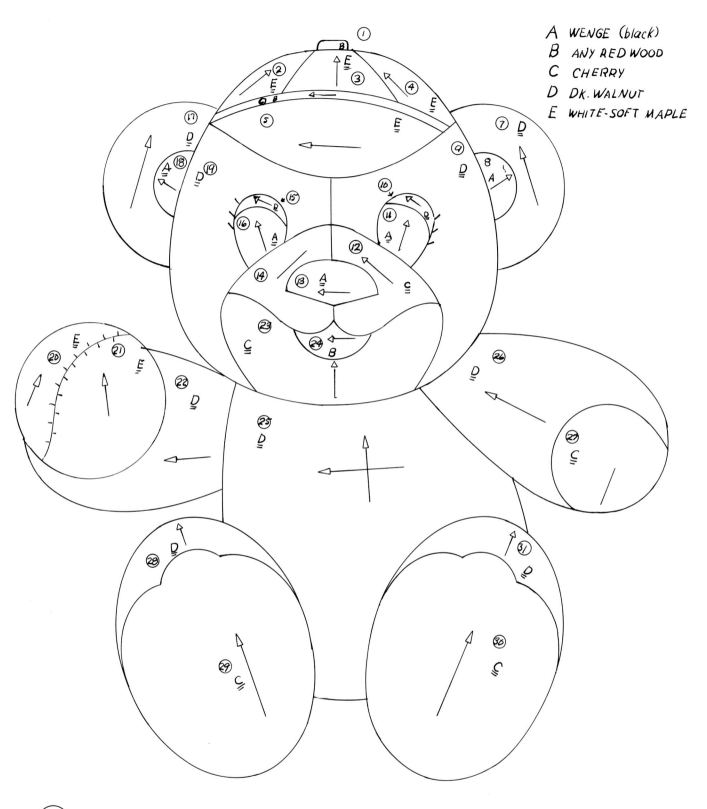

A WENGE (black)
B ANY RED WOOD
C CHERRY
D DK. WALNUT
E WHITE-SOFT MAPLE

Ⓒ 4-1993 LUCILLE CRABTREE   "BASEBALL SAM"

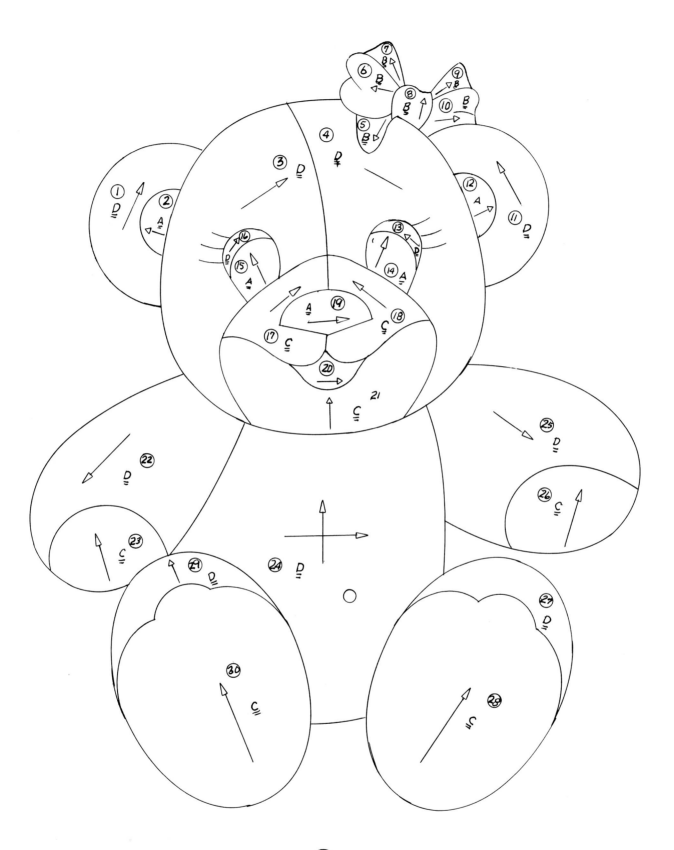

#159 4-93 PRISILLA BEAR

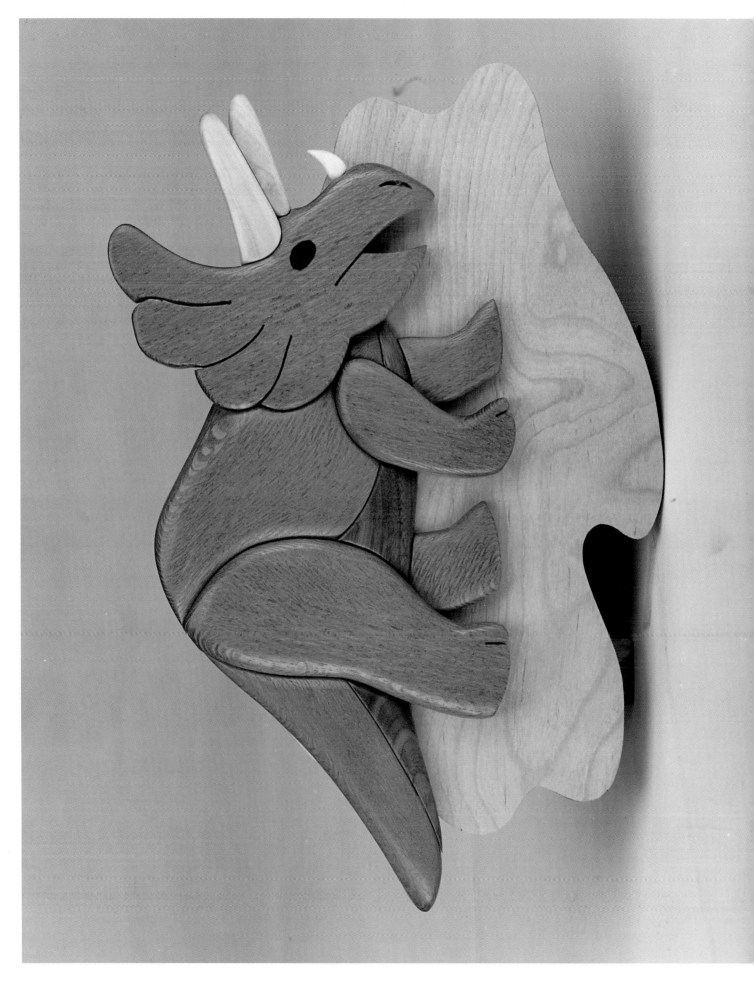

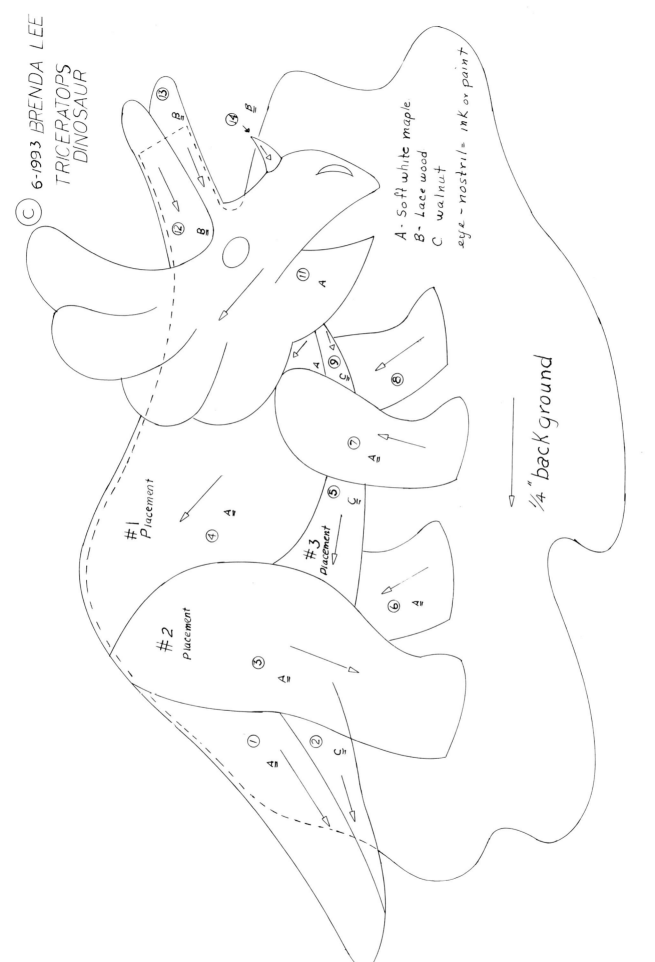

© 6-1993 BRENDA LEE
TRICERATOPS
DINOSAUR

A - Soft white maple
B - Lace wood
C - walnut
eye - nostril = ink or paint

¼" background

#1 Placement
#2 Placement
#3 Placement

63

More to Come...

Intarsia

This book presents a large-scale project for intarsia enthusiasts: a lazy lion stretched out in the sun! Detailed, step-by-step instructions will explain how to select varieties of wood, how to use a pattern, how to cut and shape pieces, how to fit them together precisely, and how to finish your piece. Crabtree gives many "insider's secrets" for making sure that your pieces align correctly, and for choosing the best contours and finishes. While even a novice to intarsia will find that Crabtree's tips make their projects fit better and look more professional, this book is absolutely necessary for anyone who wishes to move on to more advanced intarsia techniques. With this book, you will learn the subtleties of "painting with wood," creating beautiful three-dimensional pictures with pieces in different colors and varieties of wood.

from Schiffer Publishing